■ SCHOLASTIC
News
Nonfiction Readers

Math in the Car

by Ellen Weiss

Children's Press®
A Division of Scholastic Inc.
New York Toronto London Auckland Sydney
Mexico City New Delhi Hong Kong
Danbury, Connecticut

These content vocabulary word builders are for grades 1–2.

Math Consultant: Linda K. Voges, EdD, Cohort Coordinator/Lecturer,
College of Education, The University of Texas at Austin

Reading Consultant: Cecilia Minden-Cupp, PhD, Early Literacy Consultant and Author,
Chapel Hill, North Carolina

Photographs © 2008: age fotostock/Javier Larrea: 15; Alamy Images: cover top inset (Kathleen Nelson),
5 top left, 11 top (Jim West), 7 (Janine Wiedel Photolibrary); Corbis Images: cover bottom inset (Ron
Chapple Stock), cover (Goodshoot); James Levin Studios: 2, 5 bottom right, 19; Masterfile/F. Lukasseck: 13;
ShutterStock, Inc.: 4 bottom right, 5 top right, 9 (JustASC), 11 bottom (Wade H. Massie); Superstock, Inc.:
back cover, 21 (age fotostock), cover center inset (Photodisc), 1, 4 bottom left, 5 bottom left, 17 (Liz Strenk).
Illustrations by Kathy Petelinsek

Book Design: Simonsays Design!
Book Production: The Design Lab

Library of Congress Cataloging-in-Publication Data
Weiss, Ellen, 1949–
Math in the car / by Ellen Weiss.
    p. cm.—(Scholastic news nonfiction readers)
Includes bibliographical references and index.
ISBN-13: 978-0-531-18530-8 (lib.bdg) 978-0-531-18783-8 (pbk)
ISBN-10: 0-531-18530-3 (lib.bdg) 0-531-18783-7 (pbk)
1. Mathematics—Juvenile literature. 2. Automobiles—Juvenile
    literature. I. Title. II. Series.
QA40.5.W445 2008
510—dc22   2007005696

CONTENTS

WORD HUNT

Look for these words as you read. They will be in **bold**.

$$220 + 9 = ?$$

add
(ad)

maximum
(**mak**-suh-muhm)

needle
(**nee**-duhl)

gas stations
(gas **stay**-shuns)

gauge
(gayj)

speed limit
(speed **li**-mut)

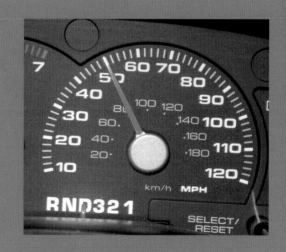

speedometer
(spi-**dah**-muh-tur)

Get Going with Math

When we take a ride in the car, there are numbers all around us.

We're going to take a trip to see Aunt Amy.

Math will help us every mile of the way.

EXIT 24

30

Newton
Wayland

1/4 ⬇ MILE

EXIT 25

INTERSTATE
90

Mass. Pike ↗

You can see many signs with
numbers along a highway.

Uh-oh, look at the gas **gauge**.

The **needle** is almost on the E for empty.

That means we're almost out of gas!

We need to fill up our gas tank.

We see 2 **gas stations**.

At 1 station, gas costs $2.00 per gallon. At the other, it costs $2.50 per gallon.

We want to buy gas for the lowest price. Which station should we choose?

How much money will we save on 1 gallon of gas?

Turn to page 23 for the answer.

$2.50 - $2.00 = ?

Food mart

Regular
unleaded
Self

2.00

2.50

Now we're back on the road. We like to look out the windows as we drive.

Sometimes we see animals.

I see 1 brown horse and 1 red barn!

How many windows do you see on the barn?

Turn to page 23 for the answer.

We see how fast we can count things as we go by.

Look at all those sheep!

Quick, count them!

How many sheep do you see?

Turn to page 23 for the answer.

15

Mom doesn't like to drive too fast.

She likes to drive at or under the **speed limit**.

The speed limit is the **maximum** speed allowed on a road.

The maximum speed allowed on this road is 65 miles per hour.

SPEED LIMIT 65

MINIMUM 40

A **speedometer** shows how fast a car is going.

This speedometer shows the speed Mom is driving.

What number is the needle pointing to?

Is it more or less than the speed limit?

Remember, the speed limit is 65 miles (105 kilometers) per hour.

Turn to page 23 for the answer.

speedometer

We've driven 220 miles (354 kilometers).

We have 9 miles (15 km) to go.

Add the two numbers together. What number do you get?

The answer is the number of miles between our house and Aunt Amy's house.

It's a long trip!

Turn to page 23 for the answer.

Lee 9
Albany 53

220 + 9 = ?

add (ad) to find the sum of two or more numbers

gas stations (gas **stay**-shuns) places that sell gasoline and other products that help keep cars running

gauge (gayj) an instrument for measuring something, such as how much gas is in a gas tank

maximum (**mak**-suh-muhm) the greatest possible amount; the upper limit of something

needle (**nee**-duhl) a pointer on a measuring instrument such as a speedometer or compass

speed limit (speed **li**-mut) the highest speed the law allows drivers to drive on a particular road

speedometer (spi-**dah**-muh-tur) an instrument in a car or other vehicle that shows how fast you are traveling

ANSWERS

Page 10
$2.50 – $2.00 = 50¢
We will save **50** cents.

Page 13
We can see **4** windows on the barn.

Page 14
There are **7** sheep.

Page 18
The needle on the speedometer is pointing to 50 miles per hour (80 kilometers per hour).
65 – 50 = 15
Our speed is 15 miles per hour (25 kilometers per hour) less than the speed limit.

Page 20
We will travel 229 miles (369 kilometers) today.
220 miles + 9 miles = 229 miles.

INDEX

FIND OUT MORE
Book:
Sargent, Brian. *Places Along the Way.* New York: Children's Press, 2007.

Website:
Coolmath.com—The Number Monster
www.coolmath-games.com/numbermonster/index.html

MEET THE AUTHOR
Ellen Weiss has received many awards for her books for kids. She lived in England for a short time, where people say "maths" instead of "math."